THE BEST DAY OF THE WEEK

Why We Love the Lord's Day

William Boekestein

illustrated by Brian Hartwell

Reformation Heritage Books
Grand Rapids, Michigan

Reformation Heritage Books
3070 29th St. SE
Grand Rapids, MI 49512
616-977-0889
orders@heritagebooks.org
www.heritagebooks.org

Scripture taken from the New King James Version®. Copyright © 1982 by Thomas Nelson. Used by permission. All rights reserved.

Printed in the United States of America
22 23 24 25 26 27/10 9 8 7 6 5 4 3 2 1

Library of Congress Cataloging-in-Publication Data

Names: Boekestein, William, author. | Hartwell, Brian, illustrator.
Title: The best day of the week : why we love the Lord's Day / William Boekestein ; illustrated by Brian Hartwell.
Description: Grand Rapids, Michigan : Reformation Heritage Books, [2022] | Audience: Ages 2-7
Identifiers: LCCN 2021049648 | ISBN 9781601789198 (hardcover)
Subjects: LCSH: Sunday—Juvenile literature. | BISAC: RELIGION / Christianity / General | RELIGION / Christian Living / Devotional
Classification: LCC BV130 .B64 2022 | DDC 263/.3—dc23/eng/20211130
LC record available at https://lccn.loc.gov/2021049648

For additional Reformed literature, request a free book list from Reformation Heritage Books at the above regular or email address.

To our parents,

for teaching us the beauty of the Lord's Day

—WB, BH

———

I was glad when they said to me,
"Let us go into the house of the LORD."

—PSALM 122:1

Hi! I've been going to worship for as long as I can remember. I'm still young, so I don't know everything, but I'd like to tell you a few things I know about this special meeting time with God. Every Sunday is a little different. So is every congregation and every family. But I'll tell it like it usually is for our family. To tell the whole Sunday story, I have to start on Saturday evening.

"Kids, it's almost bedtime. Come upstairs for a bath."
Even before we hear Mom's voice, we know it's bath
time when we hear water crashing into the tub.

"Is it bedtime already?" That's my little sister. She sometimes for-
gets that we should be clean and well rested for meeting God on
Sunday morning.

After bath time, we always pile on the sofa for family worship. All the readers in the family read a few verses from the Bible, and Dad helps us understand what we've read. After reading the Bible, we sing a song together before prayer time. "That's the way to end a day!" says Dad as he kisses us goodnight.

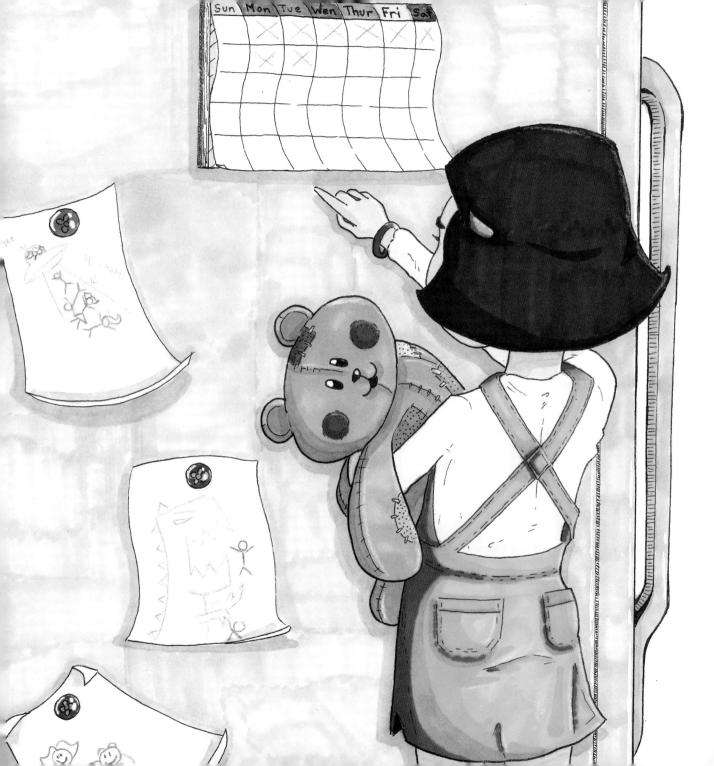

One of my little sisters always asks on Sunday mornings, "Is it worship day today?" Somehow, she always seems to know. The day just feels different from the others. And it is. The fourth commandment says we must "remember the Sabbath day, to keep it holy" (Ex. 20:8). "Holy" means special. God's special day reminds us that Jesus rose from the dead for our salvation. It also helps us to think about the rest that God will give His children in heaven.

We go to bed early on Saturday so we can wake up on Sunday not feeling too tired or being too rushed to get ready. One time I forgot breakfast and my stomach growled so loudly that I think it frightened people. What do you like to eat in the morning?

After Dad parks the car, we all pile out and make our way toward the front door of the church building.

"Good morning," says Mr. Johnson. Mr. Johnson is a greeter. He makes sure that everyone who gathers for worship is welcomed with a smile. He helps us be glad to be in God's house (Ps. 122:1). Even though we are happy to meet with God, we never forget that He is a great King (Ps. 95:3).

"Okay, everyone, time to use the bathroom," whispers Mom. "I don't have to go," one of my sisters says. I don't want to say too much about it, but I've learned the hard way not to take any chances.

When it's time to be seated, Mr. Painter, the usher, hands us each a bulletin. The bulletin helps us know what is going to happen during the service. It also tells us about events in the life of the congregation and gives us ideas for prayer. Mr. Painter walks our family down the aisle and helps us find a seat. Time for me to take a break from thinking about all the projects I am working on, and my tree fort, and my sandbox—and think about God.

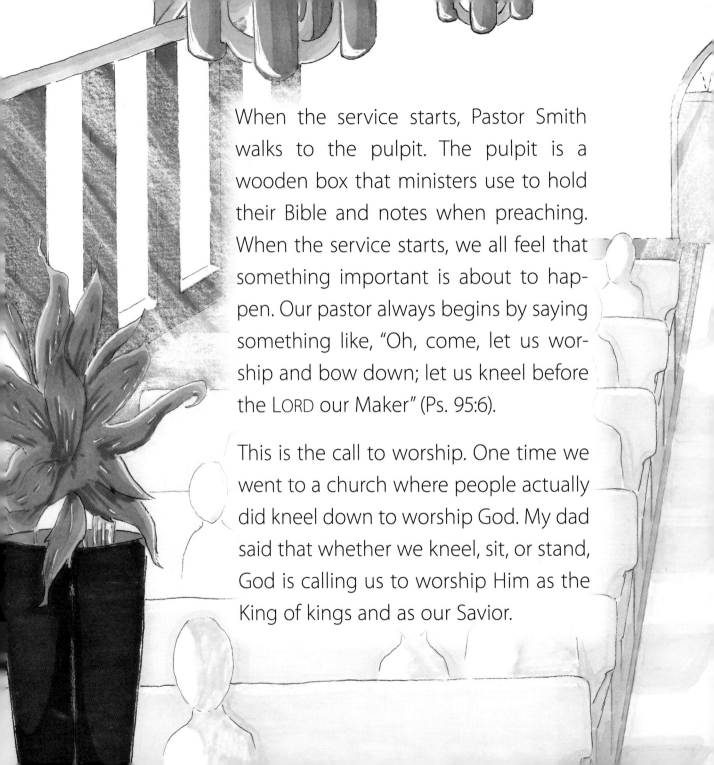

When the service starts, Pastor Smith walks to the pulpit. The pulpit is a wooden box that ministers use to hold their Bible and notes when preaching. When the service starts, we all feel that something important is about to happen. Our pastor always begins by saying something like, "Oh, come, let us worship and bow down; let us kneel before the LORD our Maker" (Ps. 95:6).

This is the call to worship. One time we went to a church where people actually did kneel down to worship God. My dad said that whether we kneel, sit, or stand, God is calling us to worship Him as the King of kings and as our Savior.

Because meeting with God is so important, our pastor always reminds us that "our help is in the name of the LORD, who made heaven and earth" (Ps. 124:8).

Pastor Smith then raises his arms higher than everyone's heads and says, "Grace to you and peace from God our Father and the Lord Jesus Christ" (1 Cor. 1:3). The bulletin calls this the salutation. I used to think this was just our pastor's way of saying hello. But now I know that God greets His people in a special way through the minister.

Near the beginning of the service, our minister reads God's law, which tells us that we sin and fall short of God's glory (Rom. 3:23). This is bad news. But it helps us confess to God how we have sinned and ask for His forgiveness. Our minister also always reads the good news, what the Bible calls the gospel: God saves sinners who trust in Him. God saw everything His trusting children did all week and loves them even if some of those things were wrong! Sometimes we use very old words to speak our faith aloud. The Apostles' Creed reminds us that God the Father, God the Son, and God the Holy Spirit work together to give God's children eternal life.

The longest part of the church service is the sermon. It is long, my dad says, because God has a lot to say about Himself and His gift of Jesus. Our pastor helps us to understand the Bible so we can obey what it says with hearts that trust Jesus. To keep from daydreaming, I write down some of the words the minister says or draw a picture about a story our pastor told in the sermon. I also try to remember questions to ask my parents about things from the sermon I didn't understand. Sometimes I can tell that Pastor Smith is talking right to me. Like when he said, "Children, just as Jesus held other little children and blessed them (Mark 10:16), He will care for you if you ask Him for His help."

Sometimes we celebrate sacraments. My dad says they are stories of God's grace in pictures. When I was very little, I didn't understand why in the Lord's Supper the elders served pieces of bread and wine. My dad explained that God feeds His children's faith through the bread and wine, which are like the body and blood of Christ which He offered on the cross. This small meal teaches us to look forward to the banquet God will serve His friends after Jesus comes again. The other sacrament is baptism. Baptism uses water to show that God loves His people and washes away their sins.

One of my favorite parts of worshiping God is the singing. Even when I was very little, I would hold the songbook (sometimes upside down!) and try to hum along. Singing is like praying with music. Sometimes we pray without music. Our pastor helps us bring our praise, fears, sins, and needs to God. While the pastor prays, we pray with him. But most importantly we pray with Jesus, who lives to help us (Heb. 7:25). Isn't it great to know that God hears the prayers of His children?

Before the end of the service, we get to put money in the collection plate to show that we are thankful to God for His grace. I wonder if I'll ever find out how God used my quarters for His glory.

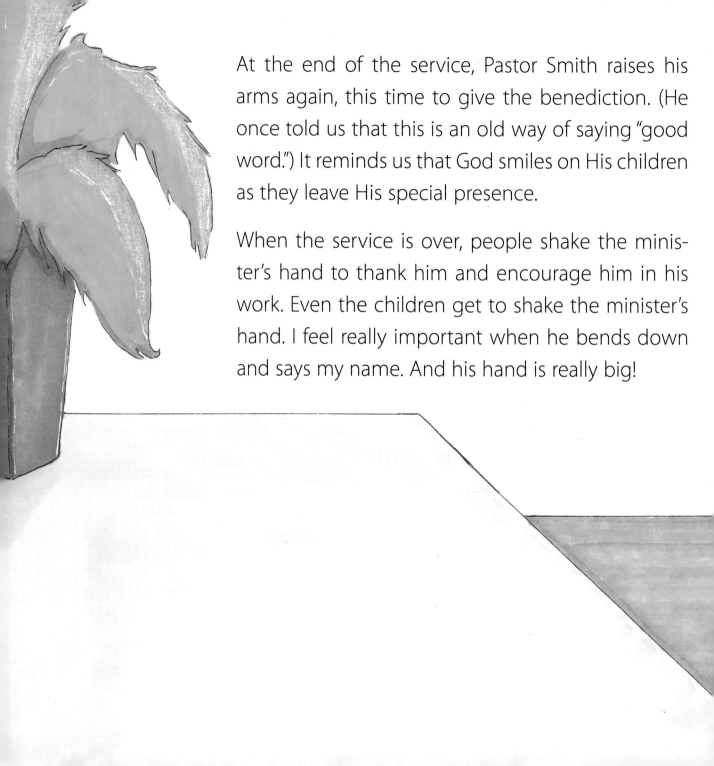

At the end of the service, Pastor Smith raises his arms again, this time to give the benediction. (He once told us that this is an old way of saying "good word.") It reminds us that God smiles on His children as they leave His special presence.

When the service is over, people shake the minister's hand to thank him and encourage him in his work. Even the children get to shake the minister's hand. I feel really important when he bends down and says my name. And his hand is really big!

The drive home after the service is a great time for our family to talk about what happened during worship. I always know what my dad is going to ask as soon as we've pulled onto the street: "Okay kids, what did you learn about God and His amazing grace this morning?" Good thing I took notes!

Proverbs 20:11 says, "Even a child is known by his deeds." With God's help even children can start doing what God wants. And the best time to start is right away, while His word is fresh in our minds.

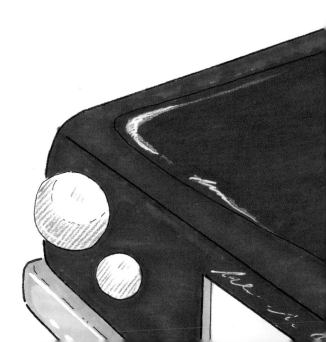

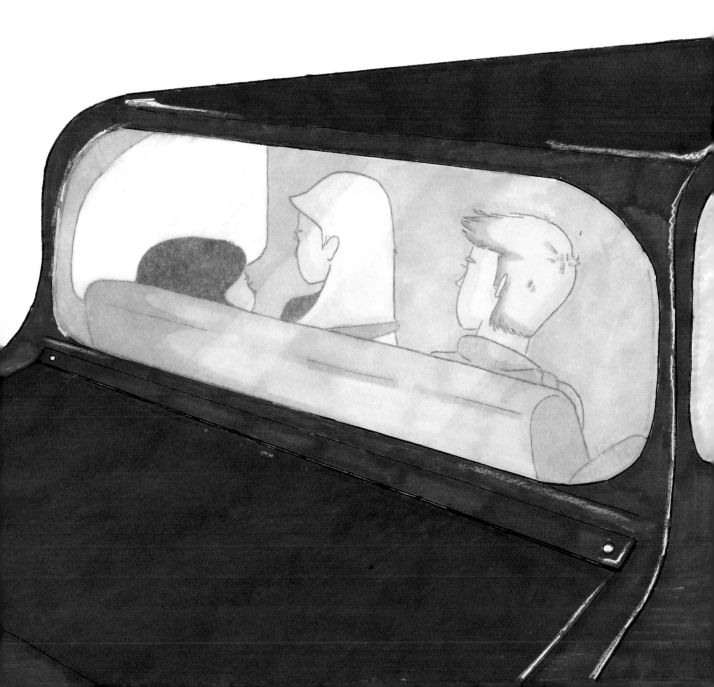

Since Sunday is a day of rest from our usual jobs, we get to spend the afternoon together as a family before going back to church for another service. Sometimes we share meals with other church friends and visitors we have just met. I have made a lot of friends this way!

Since Sunday helps us get ready to be with the Lord, it is the best day to feed our souls the way food feeds our bodies. Watching videos about Christian missionaries shows us how God is working around the

world. Reading books like *Pilgrim's Progress* teaches us how to advance toward heaven. Singing and reading the Bible together helps us use this special day to glorify and enjoy God.

I've learned to love the Lord's Day, and I hope you will, too. It helps me trust in Jesus and get ready to live for God every day. I agree with a song we sing: "Day of all the week the best, emblem of eternal rest." Sunday is the best day of the week!

NOTE TO PARENTS

Since you are reading these words, I feel confident surmising a few things about you. One, you believe that all people are worshipers. It is not a question of *if* we worship but of *what*, *who*, and *how* we worship. This is true for both adults and children. Two, you want your children or other children you love to join the great cloud of witnesses in worshiping the true God according to His Word. You aren't convinced that children should be segregated from the rest of the congregation but are assured that they, as members of God's family, are fully capable with His help of worshiping Him (Matt. 21:15). Three, you are looking for all the help you can get in this monumental calling! We hope this book will help your children better understand congregational worship and give you an opportunity to personalize Jesus's invitation: "Let the little children come to Me" (Mark 10:14). Here are a few additional words of encouragement to help you in your eternally valuable quest.

Train your children at home.

Expecting any child to sit reasonably still and quiet in church—and no church should expect children to be statues in worship—can feel intimidating. But expecting children to do so only once a week without any practice at home is wishful thinking. Regular family worship—a simple routine of Bible reading, discussion, singing, and prayer—is the best primer for congregational worship and a crucial opportunity to nurture God's children toward spiritual maturity.

Facilitate participation at church.

Children should never be mere observers in the service. You can help them participate in the service of worship by explaining what is happening and encouraging their memorization and recitation of repeated worship elements like the Lord's Prayer and the doxology. Teach them to listen to the prayers and the preaching. Have them help you give the offering. Talk them through the meaning behind baptism and the Lord's Supper (Ex. 13:14).

Be positive and patient.

In the second commandment, God announces a curse on the generations of those who fail to worship Him rightly; He promises blessings to the generations of loving, obedient worshipers. God is dropping a clue: worship rituals are passed on generationally. Worship, biblical or unbiblical, creates a lasting impression on young hearts and minds (Prov. 22:6). Discipline may be occasionally necessary. But never lose sight of this goal: you want your children to sense that joining the congregation in praising God is the most positive, life-giving experience in the world.

Read books that encourage and equip you.

Four excellent books on this subject are Joel Beeke's *The Family at Church: Listening to Sermons and Attending Prayer Meetings*; Robbie Castleman's *Parenting in the Pew: Guiding Your Children into the Joy of Worship*; Jason Helopoulos's *Let the Children Worship*; and Daniel R. Hyde's *The Nursery of the Holy Spirit: Welcoming Children in Worship*.